A CHILD'S DAY
IN A VIETNAMESE CITY

For Thanh and Katy

Benchmark Books
Marshall Cavendish
99 White Plains Road
Tarrytown, NY 10591
www.marshallcavendish.com

Library of Congress Cataloging-in-Publication Data

Morgan, Tom, 1975-
In a Vietnamese city / [text] by Tom Morgan and
[photographs by] Jim Holmes.--1st American ed.
p. cm. -- (A child's day)
Includes bibliographical references and index.
Summary: Presents a day in the life of two brothers living in Danang, discussing
the social life, customs, religion, history, and language of Vietnam.
ISBN 0-7614-1409-6
1. Vietnam--Social life and customs--Juvenile literature. 2. Children--Vietnam--Juvenile literature. 3.
City and town life--Vietnam--Juvenile literature. [1. Vietnam--Social life and customs.] I. Holmes, Jim, ill.
II. Title. III. Series.
DS559.93.D34 M67 2002   959.7--dc21   2001007577

Designed by Sophie Pelham

Printed in Singapore

1 3 5 7 9 8 6 4 2

AUTHOR ACKNOWLEDGMENTS
Many thanks to the Lê family, particularly Huy and Vinh, for their assistance with this project and for their generosity.

A CHILD'S DAY
IN A VIETNAMESE CITY

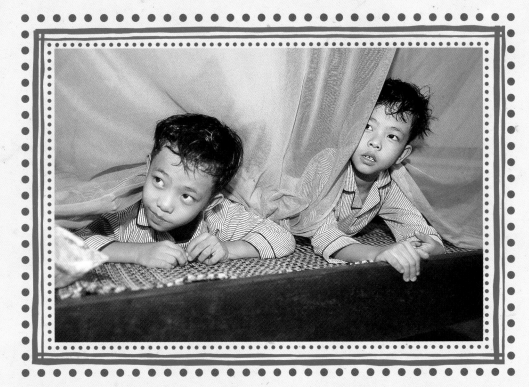

Jim Holmes and Tom Morgan

Benchmark Books

MARSHALL CAVENDISH
NEW YORK

AUTHOR'S NOTE

Huy and Vinh live in the city of Danang, which lies halfway down Vietnam's long coastline. The streets of Danang are always buzzing with the sounds of people doing their shopping, chatting with their friends over noodle soup, or lining up to get their bicycles fixed. If all the noise stopped for a moment, the people on the streets would probably be able to hear the whoosh of the great Han River, winding its way through the center of the city. They might even look up and admire the Son Tra mountains beyond.

Many Vietnamese are farmers who work in rice fields and live in small villages, but the people who live in towns and cities like Danang have other kinds of jobs. Danang is a port, so many local people work on the ships that arrive daily, bringing oil and leaving with coal and seafood.

No matter what part of the country they come from, most Vietnamese love having guests. If you came to visit, you might be invited to someone's house for *trà* (tea), or perhaps even a meal.

Danang

VIETNAM

Huy and Vinh are seven years old.

They live with their parents and older sister, Nhi, in a single-story house on the outskirts of Danang. They share their busy city with more than a million other people. The children's father, Xuan, is the manager of a local bank, and their mother, Tam, is a dressmaker.

Huy and Vinh begin their day at six o'clock. Today is the anniversary of their great-grandfather's death, so they make offerings of biscuits and fruit at the family's *bàn thờ* (ancestral shrine) outside in the yard. Then they burn incense sticks and pray to their great-grandfather for his help and protection.

Most Vietnamese believe that their family members live on as spirits after they have died, and that it is important to show them respect.

Back inside the house the twins take a shower and change into their school uniforms.

They have just enough time for a quick cup of *sữa* (milk) before their mother says they have to leave for school.

Huy and Vinh walk
toward school with their
mother, while their father
heads to work on his
xe gắn máy (motorbike).

*XE GẮN MÁY Small motorbikes are
extremely popular in Vietnam and
most families have at least one.
Cars are rare, but it is not unusual
to see many people traveling on the
same motorbike!*

Before they go into school, the twins and their mother meet up with Nhi at a nearby breakfast stand. The stand sells two types of rice noodle soup: *phở* and *bún*. Huy and Vinh each have a bowl of *bún*, the spicier version. Vietnamese usually buy their breakfast soup from a stand because it would take too long to prepare it at home.

When they have finished their soup, Huy, Vinh, and Nhi go in through the school gates. Like most schools in Vietnam, *Phù Đổng* is very large—there are more than two thousand students in all.

PHÙ ĐỔNG is the hero of a well-known Vietnamese legend. According to the legend, Phù Đổng was only three years old when he defended his country against Chinese invaders. His first words to his mother were a request to prepare him for battle!

Before lessons start at seven o'clock, the twins chat with their friends. They stay in the shade of the school buildings and the *cây vung đống* (shade tree) because it is already hot, even at this time of the morning.

The first lesson of the day is Vietnamese. The teacher reads the class a story about a poor rice farmer who gives shelter to a stranger who is even poorer than himself. Many years later, the stranger returns as a wealthy man and is able to help the farmer in return for his kindness.

The second lesson is science. Today the class is learning how to measure temperature. Vinh is asked to come up to the blackboard and draw a graph showing the average monthly temperatures in Danang. He has to concentrate very hard, which isn't easy when the whole class is watching!

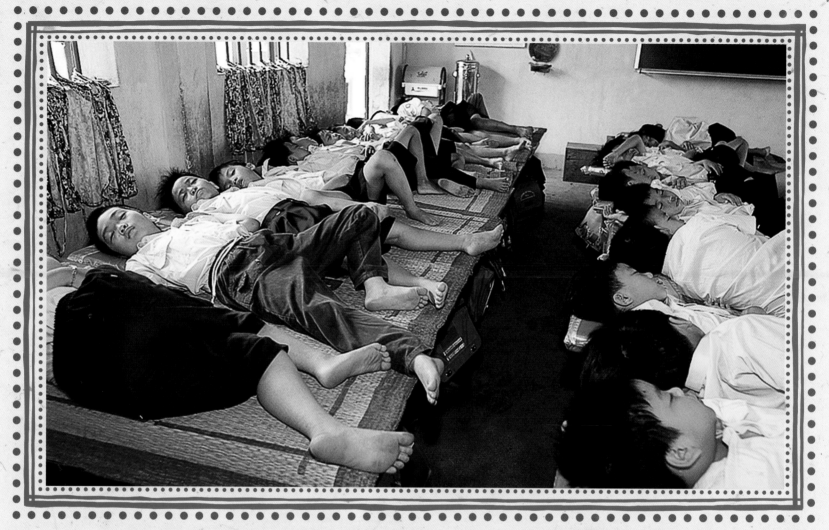

After morning lessons all the students and teachers break for lunch and then have a nap until school reopens in the afternoon. It is a long break because this is the hottest part of the day and it would be difficult to work. The children who live near the school go home, but Huy and Vinh put mats on their desks and sleep in the classroom.

The first lesson after lunch break is *môn toán* (math), Vinh's
favorite subject. Huy prefers writing stories and reading books.
He is happy to take a break from his work while the teacher shows
him how to hold his pen properly.

When lessons are over, Tam and the twins go to the market. At the vegetable stand, she buys two types of gourds (which look like small pumpkins) and some *rau muống* (morning glory, a green leafy vegetable).

They ride in a *xe xích lô* (rickshaw) to go home.

On the way they pass some street vendors carrying bananas. The baskets are heavy, so the vendors balance them across their shoulders.

When the groceries have been unpacked and put away in the cupboards, they set off for a beach by the South China Sea. But first they stop for some *kem sầu riêng* (durian-flavored ice cream) as a special treat.

KEM SẦU RIÊNG is made with durian fruit, which is very popular in Southeast Asia. Durian fruit has a hard, spiky rind and an unusual smell. Many people think the smell is unpleasant, but the fruit itself tastes delicious.

At Danang beach Huy, Vinh, and Nhi dig in the sand to see if they can find any crabs. It is only safe to swim in the sea from April to September. In winter the waves are often too rough, and the water gets icy cold.

Once they get home the twins need a shower to wash all the sand out of their hair. Afterward they settle down to complete the multiplication exercises they began at school. Vinh finishes his first and then helps his brother.

Then they run out to the yard and play *bóng đá* (soccer) with their friends Diep and Phuong.

BÓNG ĐÁ Vietnamese children often play soccer in the garden or on the streets. It is not taught at school because there isn't usually space on the school grounds for a playing field. Vietnamese schoolchildren do exercises every day instead.

While the twins play outside, Tam goes back to work at her shop. Tam is an expert dressmaker. She makes her *máy may* (sewing machine) go so fast, it is impossible to see the needle as it stitches the fabrics together.

Today is *Tết Trung Thu*, the Vietnamese mid-autumn festival. To help them celebrate, the twins' father has given them some *bánh trung thu*, a star-shaped lantern, and some masks to wear. The masks represent the Vietnamese god of the land, who has the power to drive away evil spirits.

BÁNH TRUNG THU are special festival cakes. They are made out of sticky rice, fruit, and nuts or lotus seeds. If your bánh trung thu is square, it symbolizes the earth, and if it is round, it symbolizes the moon.

23

When Tam gets back from her shop, she changes into her cooking clothes and starts preparing the *rau muống*, the vegetable that she bought earlier at the market. She wants her children to eat lots of vegetables so that they stay healthy.

She also cooks red fish in a sweet onion and black pepper sauce.

24

Tam has cooked more than usual this evening because the children's grandparents are having dinner with them. Besides the *rau muống* and the fish, they eat boiled chicken and patties made from pork and herbs. Each dish is placed on the table so that the family can serve themselves.

After dinner they play Grandma's favorite game, *cờ cá ngựa*.

CỜ CÁ NGỰA is a board game about horse racing. Each player has a team of four horses and the aim is to get your team to the finish line before anyone else does. If your horse lands on the same spot as someone else's, you can "kick" that player's horse right back to the beginning of the course.

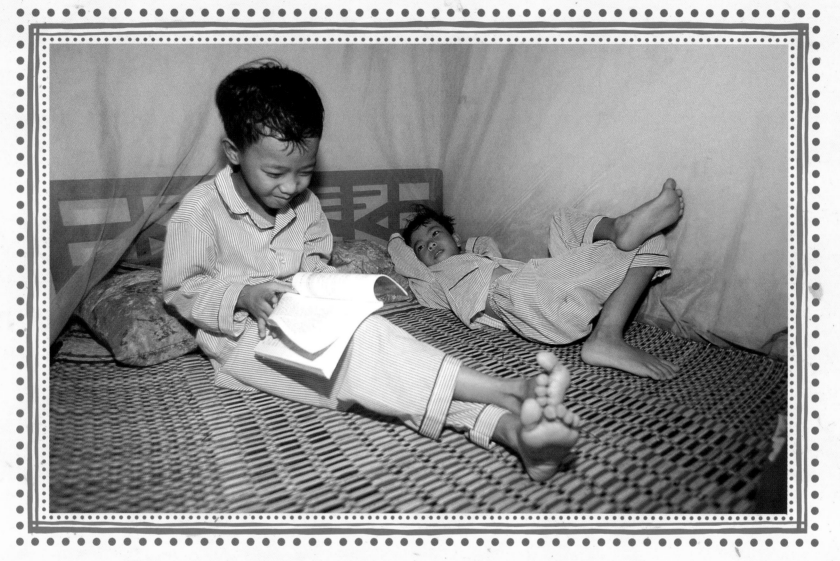

By about nine o'clock the twins are ready for bed. Huy is sleepy after his busy day, so he asks Vinh to turn off the light and save his book until tomorrow. *Chúc Huy và Vinh ngủ ngon.* (Good night, Huy and Vinh.)

MORE ABOUT VIETNAM

VIETNAM, THE LAND

Vietnam is a very long, thin country in Southeast Asia, shaped like the letter *S*. It is wide in the north and the south but thin in the middle—at its thinnest point it is only thirty miles across.

Outside the cities much of Vietnam is covered by bright green paddy fields, where rice is grown. Rice is the staple food of Vietnam, which means it is eaten at almost every meal. The farmers who work in the paddy fields wear conical hats made from woven leaves to protect themselves from the sun and the rain. Although the weather in Vietnam varies from month to month, Vietnamese farmers divide the year into two main seasons: the dry season and the wet season.

VIETNAM, THE PAST

The Vietnamese sometimes say that they have been at war for two thousand years! Many of the countries that Vietnam has fought against—including China, France, Japan, and Cambodia—have wanted to control Vietnam (or parts of it). The Vietnamese have had to battle hard for their independence.

Vietnam was ruled by the French for nearly a hundred years, until the Vietnamese—led by their most famous leader, Ho Chi Minh—fought a war to make the French leave. When the French had been driven out in 1954, Vietnam split into North Vietnam and South Vietnam. The two parts had very different types of government and did not agree on how to treat the Vietnamese people. The United States decided to help South Vietnam fight North Vietnam, leading to the Vietnam War. Eventually North Vietnam gained control of South Vietnam, and Vietnam became a united country again. These days Vietnam is finally at peace and is developing quickly.

RELIGION IN VIETNAM

Some Vietnamese are Christians, but most follow a mixture of three different religions: Buddhism, which came to Vietnam from India, and Confucianism and Taoism, which both came from China. Almost every Vietnamese home has a shrine where people can make offerings of flowers and fruit for good luck and protection. Many Vietnamese also worship their ancestors, which means that they honor family members who have died. They usually have a separate shrine where they display photographs of their ancestors, and they make offerings of their ancestors' favorite foods once a year.

PEOPLE IN VIETNAM

Most Vietnamese are members of the same ethnic group, but there are also many hill peoples who live in the highlands in the central and northern parts of the country. These peoples have their own beliefs, customs, and languages.

Many of Vietnam's artists, writers, and poets come from North Vietnam, while South Vietnam is famous for its business people and traders. No matter which part of the country they come from, many Vietnamese have a reputation for working hard. It is not unusual for shops to stay open for eighteen hours a day, because the shopkeepers want to do as much business as possible.

Family relationships are very important in Vietnam. The Vietnamese believe that the older you are the more you should be respected, so grandparents are considered the most important members of the family. It is traditional for lots of family members to live together, and people often continue living in the same house after they are married. This means that houses in Vietnam can be very crowded, but nobody seems to mind.

LANGUAGE IN VIETNAM

Nearly everyone in Vietnam speaks Vietnamese, although the groups of people who live in the highlands have their own languages. There are also many Chinese people in Vietnam, and they usually speak Chinese within their own communities. Vietnamese is spoken with different accents around the country, so you can tell where someone comes from as soon as he or she starts to speak.

A long time ago Vietnamese writing was made up of symbols called characters, which were similar to the characters used in Chinese writing. But modern Vietnamese writing looks more like English, because it uses the same alphabet that we do. Most Asian languages—such as Chinese and Japanese—use characters rather than letters, so Vietnamese is unusual. Although Vietnamese has the same letters as English, it also uses special marks to help the reader know how to say the words correctly.

Vietnamese is a tonal language. This means that the same word can have different meanings, depending on how it is said. The word *Tam*, which is the twins' mother's name, is a good example. *Tam* can also mean "to take a shower" or "eight," and in old Vietnamese, *tam* means "three"!

Most Vietnamese children learn English at school because this will help them talk to people from different countries around the world when they get older. Some children also learn French.

SOME VIETNAMESE WORDS AND PHRASES

xin chào (sin chow)—hello

cám ơn (cam urn)—thank you

Bạn đi đâu đó? (bang dee doe dor)—
  Where are you going? (a common greeting used instead of hello)

tạm biệt (tam bia)—good-bye

THE VIETNAMESE WORDS IN THE BOOK

bàn thờ—many Vietnamese have shrines in their homes so that they can make offerings of food and drink to their ancestors, and pray to them for guidance and help. People often place photographs of these ancestors on the shrine so that they can look at them while they are praying. Even though they are no longer alive, the ancestors are still thought of as important members of the family.

bánh trung thu—the special cakes that are eaten during the Vietnamese mid-autumn festival

bóng đá—soccer

bún—a spicy rice noodle soup that is eaten for breakfast

cây vung đống—the name given to any tree in Danang that creates a lot of shade

Chúc Huy và Vinh ngủ ngon—Good night, Huy and Vinh

cờ cá ngựa—a board game about horse racing

kem sầu riêng—durian-flavored ice cream

máy may—sewing machine

môn toán—math

phở—a rice noodle soup that is eaten for breakfast

Phù Đổng—the hero of a Vietnamese legend who defended his country against the Chinese when he was only three years old. The twins' school is called *Phù Đổng* in his honor.

rau muống—morning glory, a green leafy vegetable

sữa—milk

Tết Trung Thu—the Vietnamese mid-autumn festival, also known as Children's Day. It is celebrated on the fourteenth or fifteenth day of the eighth lunar month. This means that it falls on a different date every year, but it is always some time during September or October.

trà—tea

xe gắn máy—motorbike

xe xích lô—rickshaw

FIND OUT MORE

Brittan, Dolly. *The People of Vietnam*. New York: Rosen Publishing Group, 1997.

Dahl, Michael S. *Vietnam*. Mankato, Minnesota: Capstone Press, 1998.

O'Connor, Karen. *Vietnam*. Minneapolis, Minnesota: Lerner, 1999.

INDEX